Burning Wyclif

THE WALT MCDONALD FIRST-BOOK
SERIES IN POETRY

Robert A. Fink, *editor*

Burning Wyclif

THOM SATTERLEE

Introduction by Robert Fink

Texas Tech University Press

This book is typeset in Scala. The paper used in this book meets the minimum requirements of ANSI/NISO Z39.48-1992 (R1997). ∞

Designed by Barbara Werden

LIBRARY OF CONGRESS CATALOGING-IN-PUBLICATION DATA
Satterlee, Thom.
Burning Wyclif / Thom Satterlee ; introduction by Robert Fink.
p. cm. — (The Walt McDonald first-book series in poetry)
Summary: "Fourteenth-century scholar and reformer John Wyclif is the subject and often persona of this collection of poems ranging from traditional to free verse and including some shaped like the objects they describe, an altar piece, the head of a pin. Winner of the 2005 Walt McDonald First-Book Competition in Poetry" — Provided by publisher.
Includes bibliographical references.
ISBN-13: 978-0-89672-576-8 (alk. paper)
ISBN-10: 0-89672-576-6 (alk. paper)
1. Wycliffe, John, d. 1384 — Poetry. 2. Reformation — Poetry.
3. Reformers — Poetry. I. Title. II. Series.
PS3619.A8226B87 2005
811'.6—dc22
2005026555

Printed in the United States of America
06 06 07 08 09 10 11 12 13 14 / 9 8 7 6 5 4 3 2 1
SB

Texas Tech University Press
Box 41037
Lubbock, Texas 79409-1037 USA
800.832.4042
ttup@ttu.edu
www.ttup.ttu.edu

FOR MY PARENTS,
Douglas and Virginia Satterlee

Acknowledgments

Grateful acknowledgment is made to the following periodicals—

Alaska Quarterly Review—"Wyclif Practices the Art of Definition While Walking to His Morning Class"

Anglican Theological Review—"The Lesson"

Antietam Review—"The Sense in Which Wyclif Might Be Called a Martyr"

Chrysalis Reader—"Awake in Oxford"

Crazyhorse—"One John Dies, the Other Wakes to Crickets"

Greensboro Review—"Ibn Khatir Tells How He Survived the Black Death"

Image—from "The Private Meditations of John Wyclif: On Angels," from "The Private Meditations of John Wyclif: On Celibacy" and from "The Private Meditations of John Wyclif: On the Virgin Birth"

The Lyric—"The Caretaker of St. Mary's Church Comments on Recent Scholarly Findings"

Nimrod—"A Young Italian Man Healed of the Plague by Saint Bridget of Sweden"

Notre Dame Review—"Wyclif Places Himself, His Room Within the Ten Categories of Essential Being" and "A Visit to Lutterworth"

Roanoke Review—"Brethren of the Cross: Oxford, May 19, 1349"

The Southern Review—"The Steward's Prayer Book," "Purvey Describes His Work with Wyclif," and "Purvey Translates: *In ipso enim vivimus et movemur et sumus*"

Southwest Review—"Habitus"

Spoon River Poetry Review—"Gravedigger"

Sycamore Review—"William of Ockham Visits the Sick"

West Branch—"How Wyclif Survived the Long, Hard Winter of 1363: A

Diptych" and "The Black Friars Beg Wyclif to Recant of His Chief Heresy and Die in Peace: A Triptych"

The author would also like to thank the Ludwig Vogelstein Foundation and Taylor University for their support and Ellen Vinz for her excellent copyediting.

Contents

꩜

IV: Disputations on Human Love, Bearing
Especially on a Certain Widow
of Fillingham

V: *from* The Private Meditations
of John Wyclif

Introduction

MOST of us recognize the name John Wyclif and associate it with the translation of the Latin Vulgate Bible into English. Admirers will add that Wyclif was one of the most prominent philosophers and theologians of the second half of the fourteenth century. Others will call him *heretic* for his condemnation of what he saw as corruption in the Catholic Church and especially for his attack on the Church's doctrine of transubstantiation. If we want to know the facts of Wyclif's life, we can consult an encyclopedia or a biography. If we want to know John Wyclif, and maybe ourselves, we should read Thom Satterlee's poetry collection *Burning Wyclif*. The book is structured in a chronological sequence of selected events from Wyclif's life and times, but reading the poems, drawn in by compelling voices and the confessional tone, I feel as if I am listening to a good friend sitting across from me unburdening himself, and I know it isn't just John Wyclif's story I am attending to.

I think of my friend Will Rawlins—master mechanic laying his hand upon the hood of a high-performance engine like an artist stroking a brush across a canvas, like a poet touching pen to paper. I recall George Knight, theology professor at Hardin-Simmons University, telling me what it meant to be nineteen and pulling himself through the window of his family's stockcar-circuit winner, then walking up to his father, dropping the ignition key in his palm, and turning to God. And Robert Hamner, who, owing his life to a dead man's kidney, offers each day a prayer of gratitude to the man he never met, then bends down to help his wife ease into and out of bed, into and out of automobiles, and taking her forearm and hand in his, walks her along treacherous sidewalks like young sweethearts, indifferent to pedestrians, their busy lives. I think of Mary Fisher, her ashes a libation poured out on currents rising from the canyon of her girlhood. And Sonja Clayton, lifted from the bathroom tiles by her daughters and laid upon the hospice bed with her two words, one of which is *yes*. And certainly I think of Bob Fink grown weary because, like Dylan Thomas's "wise men," his "words had forked no lightning" ("Do Not Go Gentle Into That Good Night"). And wouldn't Thom Satterlee see himself in John Wyclif? Couldn't this book be Thom Satterlee's "Song Of Myself," a song sung in unison with Walt Whitman's invitation to seize life, assume what he assumes, celebrate our invisible selves, the life defined beneath the clothing of our lives?

The title of the book prepares us for the book's chronological and thematic structure: young Wyclif shepherding lambs on his father's farm; his student years at Oxford; his refusal to look away from the commonness of suffering and death in the Plague years; his struggle with desire for a certain young widow of Fillingham; giving himself, his pen, to God and turning to writing as meditation and judgment; suffering two strokes, rushing words upon page after page after page. John Wyclif burned with passion—a man like other men; the betrayed Christ crucified, risen; a martyr metaphorically burning, heretical books tossed onto a conflagration, bones exhumed from holy ground and burned to ashes. In the final section, the poet and his wife visiting Lutterworth, St. Mary's church, slip us in as well, each of us acknowledging our communion with the dead, the click of bones a reminder: "'We were once / as you are now'" ("A Visit to Lutterworth").

It is this burning, this hunger, that drives us, like Wyclif, to know ourselves, know the Truth, questing for more, becoming *something new* ("Tonsure"). For John Wyclif theologian, this passion is to know the word which is God and the son of God, the word invisible, a *habitus*, clothing, disguising the word. For John Wyclif philosopher, the word is ourselves hidden from ourselves, not the word undressed, undisguised, but burdened with the clothing of accident, displacement, desire, prophesy, death and surviving, inspiration, our lives defined by the quality of our losses, by the dignity of body and soul. And the answer that may come for us, as it came for Wyclif at the last, is that each of us is "bound together," each "a word / in the Word of God," the word spoken "in that language / before languages . . . " ("Purvey Translates . . . ").

It might seem that *Burning Wyclif* is a dark book of death and denial, displacement and desire, but the John Wyclif in these poems is Wyclif undraped, not the word, but the sound of the word, not

> . . . the sadness of being a word—
> only one surface to show the world
> while he lived underneath the layers
> and listened for the barely audible
> sound of his own heart beating.
> —"Habitus"

The Wyclif of *Burning Wyclif* is not the shepherd, but the sheep "shorn till its skin showed" ("Tonsure"); the hungry student sighing "for our lost ones"; the young man confessing his many passions, who presses against his chest Saint Augustine's *Confessions*, certain the Saint's beating heart will "be always in his work" ("The Influence of Augustine"); the young theologian who doubts whether God is listening to prayers, the Plague taking lives too fast for the gravedigger, but prays anyway—"a silent and continuous prayer / offered up in empty air" ("The Steward's Prayer Book"). Even the gravedigger, though distraught by the rain of corpses on his head, respects the bodies of the dead and lectures Death (the carter) to be "more careful with human bones" and takes time off from his sardonic gardening to "make improvement / on the rutted road" over which the carter drives his burdens ("Gravedigger").

The persona Wyclif feels a "sympathy or kinship" with those "few who give themselves / For the many" ("Brethren of the Cross . . . "); with those who bear the weight of the Father, the Son, and the Holy Spirit upon their foreheads ("Ordination"); with those whose desire, "the longings of a human heart" ("Question 1 . . . "), shakes the body, wanting more, driving Wyclif to suffer the derisive laughter of a young widow and her lover ("Question 3 . . . "), reducing Wyclif to what we all have been—"bones and beating heart— / pitiful, raw, and promising once again / this time's the last" ("Question 4 . . . ").

And haven't we, too, grown impatient with "scholastic games," incurring the pity of barefooted angels dancing for us on the point of pins, their feet bleeding, their pain a kind of joy like our own. Is this our consolation for being foolish in desire and climbing back to our ascetic garrets to set out pen and paper and sit at the desk facing the window and wait for the spirit to take us up as if we are reed-pens, "functional and willing to be used" ("Wyclif Becomes . . . ")? Our hands, celibate, open on our lap, empty ("On Celibacy"), waiting on the dove of inspiration ("On Inspiration") like a virgin open to that which "might conceive / and bear inside her what is above her" ("On the Virgin Birth"). Doesn't our work always seem unfinished, and must we always "go on waiting" ("On the Eucharist")? Don't we, like Wyclif, creating our passion before a small window in that upper room, consider ourselves "the martyr / of would-be martyrs, the spared one / whose lungs nevertheless filled with ashes" ("The Sense in Which . . . "), our words "trapped / behind doors sealed behind other doors" ("One John Dies . . . ")? Yet we continue writing the life we remember, "a life / attached to wings, all the air / to move in, and singing in the treetops" ("One John Dies . . . ").

It is this singing that Thom Satterlee celebrates in the final section of *Burning Wyclif*, a sequence linking Wyclif to Satterlee, to us—our "communing with the dead" our poetic calling, "real / as a dream" ("A Visit to Lutterworth"), the message of the dead our *carpe diem*. Along with Thom Satterlee, we "listen and nod" ("A Visit to Lutterworth"), acknowledging our need to hurry, aware we are already nodding off, our passion cooling, our fire burning down.

ROBERT A. FINK
Abilene, Texas, 2006

I

Habitus

. . . the sound of the word is the clothing of the word.

JOHN WYCLIF
On the Truth of Holy Scripture

Habitus

> Language, he asserted, was a *habitus*. . . . What precisely he meant
> by *habitus* is not explained, but the context in which the word is
> applied to language would suggest a sense of "clothing."
>
> ANNE HUDSON, "Wyclif and the English Language"

All morning he read from a thick volume
propped on a stand. He read and he read,
and when he closed his eyes
he continued to read
until the words took off their clothes
and laid them down on a hillside
that vanished whenever a cloud
passed between it and the sun.

All his life Wyclif had wanted this:
the words undressed and he going to them,
a child to a fair, burning to see
if Faith wore her hair in a braid,
whether Why held out its hands, palms up,
and where Simony put his coins
when he stood naked in the light.

But no: Wyclif had got it all wrong.
He was not going to see the words.
They were coming to him
with their arms loaded with robes
stacked so high he couldn't see their faces,
and before he knew it, invisible hands
began measuring him with ropes
stretched between his wrist and his chest,
from his hip down to the ground,
around his waist and around his neck.

The fitting took all day. He tried on
Son and Friend, Scholar, Reformer,
Heretic; he slipped into Priest,
wore also Doctor Evangelicus
and Morning Star. Some robes
hung too loosely; others pinched his neck.

In the end, he had to wear them all
and learn the sadness of being a word—
only one surface to show the world
while he lived underneath the layers
and listened for the barely audible
sound of his own heart beating.

II

THE LESSON

[Wyclif] is not in general very communicative about himself, except
to defend himself from accusations of heresy, or occasionally to
admit to facts such as youthful arrogance in debate, or
over-eating at common table.

ANTHONY KENNY
Wyclif

The Lesson

Once, as a boy, Wyclif carried a lamb
on his shoulders. Its legs dangled
across his chest, its head bobbed above his head.

He walked with it held high through the flock
as clouds gathered, darkened. At first
the rain felt good—slow, fat drops splashing

cold against his skin while the underside
of the lamb warmed his neck. He rubbed
his face against its fine new wool.

But when thunder cracked and the sheep bolted,
the boy ran, too, tripped to one side and fell
with his whole weight on top of the lamb.

The sound of its leg when it snapped
was an echo of thunder, a noise
that entered his ear and never left,

not that long day with all its lessons,
beginning with the knife his father taught him
to run under the lamb's neck, down its belly,

and then with his own hands to remove
the word of every organ, repeating their names
as his father patiently spoke them—

heart, kidney, liver, lung—or later
when the family ate stew and the boy learned
how to laugh at jokes told at his expense,

then and years later the one lesson
that remained was a bone breaking
inside his ear, the aftersound of its splintering.

Awake in Oxford

A horn to wake the dead wakes him
and Wyclif rises to his elbows
in the semi-dark, on a straw mattress

while the old Steward passes by
with the instrument to his lips
and blows again, god-awful noise

like a goose coughing at daybreak.
It will become an old joke
in which the scholars of Balliol

first grumble at the rude awakenings,
then toss shoes at the man,
then finally steal his horn

and hide it under Wyclif's bed
because no one would suspect
the scrawny boy from up North.

But so far no one has noticed
young Wyclif, who follows them
in a line down the rough-hewn stairs

and into the common room,
to a trough filled with water.
He stands shoulder to shoulder

with strangers who will become
known to him, he to them,
and dips his hands into the water.

Tonsure

Like every new student to Oxford,
Wyclif had to sit in an oak chair
on the lawn outside his college
and bend his head for the Barber.

On the grass beside his feet
small clumps of hair as fine
as feathers stirred in the breeze.
The shears made a sound

like a gate swinging loose
on its hinges, and he wondered
what was opening for him now
as hair fell past his shoulders

and the skin on the top of his head
caught a sudden flare
of sun, as if a scab
had been exposed to air,

or like the times he'd stood
under the waterfall at home
and the pressure made it hard
for him to breathe. *Become,*

he forced himself to think,
become something new,
and he felt that whatever that was
was something he already knew

he would someday be, not
the shepherd but a sheep
shorn till its skin showed.
All day long he couldn't keep

from rubbing his bald spot.
That night under Balliol's roof,
between two sleeping strangers,
he touched his head for proof

that he wasn't home, or himself, anymore.

Wyclif Places Himself, His Room Within the Ten Categories of Essential Being

1. *Substance*

My most general genus is this: *substance*,
from which I descend through many
subaltern genera—corporeal, animate, animal—
until the word *mortal* separates me
from the angels and I fall
with pigs, oxen, horses, and birds,
all my categorical companions, till we reach
the *rational*, where I must break from them
and join my own, my specific species,
which is called *man*.

2. *Quality*

I contain such accidents as are called
inseparable: my skin, white; my eyes, blue;
my nose, the shape of an isosceles
triangle tipped on its side. To these are added
more passing traits: my age, eighteen years,
three months, twelve days; my hair,
shorn in a circular fashion about my bald head
and indicating my station, clerk-student.
Also transitory is my hunger, which dinner
(I hope it is soon) will soon vanquish.

3. *Place*

I am in the world God made
in the stench-hole called Europe
on the island of England
in the town of Oxford
within the walls of Balliol.

I am not inside my father's home.
I am not in Wyclif-on-Tees.
I am in England
in the stench-hole called Europe
in the world God made.

4. *Time*

March 17, 1347, the Feast Day
of Saint Joseph of Arimathea,
patron of gravediggers. All buried today
are buried in Christ and rise
three days, three years, or three centuries
from now. No one knows the day
or the hour. In similar fashion
the mealtimes here at Balliol Hall
remain hidden. Reports have been made
of a beef stew, but so far these are only rumors.

5. *Quantity*

Five students with heads bowed
over books. Five books. Two
tables. One window. Three
ceiling beams. Two vertical
posts. Three dogs lying
on the floor. The students belong
with the books. The tables belong
with the posts. The beams belong
with the dogs. But the window
is in a category all by itself.

6. *Position*

I am sitting at a table with a book
in front of me. On my left
is Geoffrey, and on my right
is an empty chair. Under the table
there is a dog with its muzzle
on top of my feet. We are
all of us underneath the ceiling,
itself underneath the sky. Behind me
is a door that leads to the kitchen.
I keep turning around to look.

7. *Relation*

I am a son, a brother, a nephew,
a cousin. In relation to this book,
I am its reader. In that sense,
I am related to all who read it before
or will read it later. We are book-brothers.
The author who fathered these words
is then my uncle, his words
are my cousins. The books he read
are the ancestors we tell tales about
around the fire and sigh for our lost ones.

8. *State*

He gives as an example of this,
"to be wearing a cloak." Coincidentally,
I am. It's cold, and so I wear
a black cloak over my grey robe.
And yet, why wouldn't clothing
be to the person as an accident
is to *substance*, thus categorized
under *quality*, subcategory separable?
I'm confused. And what is confusion
but a *state* every being wants out of?

9. *Passion*

It's better and worse than I imagined.
Confusion, it turns out, is a *passion*,
as, for instance, paper when it burns
is said to be undergoing a *passion*.
Anything something outside of me
causes me to be is my *passion*.
The definition extends to acts
of privation. Cold, hunger, loneliness—
these, too, are my *passions*, my many *passions*.
I am full of *passions*.

10. *Action*

This one is the simplest of all.
I stand. I pick up my book. I walk
past the table and up the staircase.
I enter the bedroom I share
with three others. I set my book
on the straw mattress where I will
(sweetest *action* of all) sleep tonight.
Then I walk back down the stairs,
sit down at the table, listen to the Steward
say grace, and (finally!) dip my bread in stew.

Wyclif Practices the Art of Definition While Walking to His Morning Class

୰

A definition is a concise statement setting forth the nature
of the thing in question.

SAINT JOHN OF DAMASCUS,
The Fount of Knowledge, Chapter VIII

A door is an opening one goes in
or comes out of. A street is a map
for the feet to follow. Snow is
moisture frozen in white clusters
and falling through clouds. Clouds are
white, gray, or black patches
sewn into the fabric of sky. The sky is
not visible today. Neither is the sun.
The invisible is the visible
temporarily concealed, as God is
and has been for thirteen centuries now,
although His light is the light we walk in.
Walking is a form of movement
peculiar to man and taking him
away from some objects and towards others.
Thus I am walking from Balliol Hall
to St. Mary's Cathedral, which is
a building where mass is sung
and lectures are given. Both are
made out of words. A word is
(according to the saint from Damascus)
a door behind which
the Spirit of Truth waits. And a door
is an opening one goes in or comes out of.

Wyclif Skips the Book on Heresy

He does, however, browse its pages,
noting the one hundred and three chapters,
each devoted to a single heresy. There is one
for the Hemerabaptists, who taught no Christian
could attain salvation unless he
bathed daily. Who needs to be told
that this is nonsense? Or that the Pepuzians
are both mad and profoundly blasphemous
when they stick brass pins
into the side of a newborn baby,
catching the blood in a bowl,
mixing in flour, and baking a host
with which to celebrate the Eucharist?
The danger, he decides, lies
not in ignorance to these perversions
but in letting one's mind
be infected by them. He sets the book aside,
unable to imagine another
more full of errors and
attributed to him.

The Influence of Augustine

Wyclif takes the Saint's *Confessions*
from a shelf and carries it,
pressed against his chest,
to a nearby table. On the way,

something happens: the cover
grows warm, a light flashes.
Then, when he opens the book,
he sees a heart in ghostly gray

there on the first page. And when he holds
all the pages in one hand
and flips them, he sees the same heart
beating and becoming a deep red.

Wyclif has no words to explain this,
but in the future he will seldom write
a paragraph without quoting from the Saint.
How else could he be sure that that heart

would be always in his work?

Wintertime in Oxford

Wyclif walks with Aristotle
pressed to one ear, Augustine
to the other—medieval muffs

for the wind and cold
until the sun returns
or he graduates to a hooded robe.

III

GRAVEDIGGER

They dug for each graveyard a huge trench, in which they laid the corpses as they arrived by hundreds at a time, piling them up tier upon tier as merchandise is stowed in a ship, each covered with a little earth, until the trench could hold no more.

GIOVANNI BOCCACCIO
The Decameron

The Steward's Prayer Book

Turned to a morning prayer for mercy
with a drawing of the Lord
stretching his arms over the heads
of ten lepers kneeling before Him,

the prayer book had lain open
on a wooden stand beside his bed
so the Steward could turn
his head and see himself

an eleventh among the company
begging to be healed. When they found him
dead, three students carried his body
out of the room and down the stairs.

Now Wyclif has come to collect
the bedclothes of the deceased
according to the Town Ordinance.
He pauses over the book, considers

for a moment *miracle*, which begins
with someone asking and depends
on a willing Lord. He knows, too,
the rest of this story, how

only one of the lepers returns
to thank Him, and Jesus's words
in reply, asking about the nine
ungratefuls and knowing (He must have!)

that they stood not far away
turning over their hands
in the presence of priests,
lifting the hems of their robes

to show the smooth skin
of their legs before dancing
out of the picture. As he balls up
a sheet, Wyclif thinks maybe

this is why so few now are healed,
the ratio of nine to one
too pathetic even for the Most Merciful.
Or maybe, he thinks, reaching

across the bed for a pillow,
dying is the newest answer
to prayer. He gathers up
the bundle, holds it to his chest

with his arms crossed, and walks
to an open window. Below
on the street others have already
released their burdens, their questions

if they had them, so Wyclif
does the same, watching as a fold
of the sheet flaps loose
like the stunted wing of a bird

dropped from the sky. He turns
to go, but wonders how to leave
the prayer book—open or closed?
then decides to leave it as it was left,

a silent and continuous prayer
offered up in empty air.

William of Ockham Visits the Sick

Today I sat beside my brother's bed
and watched him cough up blood.

He turned five handkerchiefs bright red.
Each one he waved in my direction,

so I took them and tossed them in a corner.
They should be burned, I know,

but by the power of imagination
or the delirium of this damned plague

he saw them not as rags but roses
and asked me how his garden

had got inside. I left them there
to bloom toward whatever

his mind would make them. Then walking home
in the afternoon, I was surprised

by light rain. Suddenly four decades slipped away
and my brother and I turned in circles

with our mouths open. We counted out loud
the drops we caught, a contest

he always won on the muddy street
before we sloshed home to parents, a sister, our dog.

Now the world was one mouth
too short to play the game

and I was poised to lose again.

Gravedigger

1.

They used to come in coffins with a cross
carved on the lid and piled high with flowers.
The women walked with their heads down, their loss
borne ahead of them, raised on the shoulders
of men who sometimes stumbled, almost fell.
I'd watch them from a distance, my shovel hidden
behind a tree as soon as I heard the bell.
I stood just close enough that I could listen
to the priest as he spoke words to send the dead
along their way to heaven. Sometimes I tried
to see in my mind the place where his words led,
but was more often drawn to the women who cried
around the hole I'd dug. Before they'd leave
each one would toss in a tear-soaked handkerchief.

2.

That was when the dead were grieved. They are not now.
The carter shouts profanities as he bumps
his cart across a rut. He tells me how
his load came cheap as dirt, laughs, and dumps
the bodies out: six in soiled sheets
wrapped like fish in paper. Then he turns
his empty barrow and says he's other streets
to visit. "But I'll be back soon," he warns.
"Make sure you have these seeds stuck in the ground
before it rains, or the birds can get to them."
I'm glad to see him go. With no one around
except the dead (who've mastered the art of silence)
I work in peace. My shovel and my bootsole
are all I need to dig another hole.

3.

Sometimes my work's a blur I'm glad to lose
myself in. Suddenly the dirt at my feet
has formed itself into a mound I view
from down inside a hole. I bend and keep
my shovel moving, but wonder: where did I go
that's any different from the long, blank space
the dead all occupy? And then I know
the living can be buried in their days,
an hour can be a grave, and the grave nowhere
we'd want to leave. That is until we're forced.
One time, too lost in work, I didn't hear
the carter come to the end of his usual course.
Tipping his cart at the edge of my hole he said,
"Here's more!" and dumped three bodies on my head.

4.

One day I expect I'll have to bury him.
Till then we've come to a mutual agreement:
When I'm not busy burying or digging,
I take my shovel and make improvement
on the rutted road he drives his barrow down.
I cut out roots, lift out the smaller stones;
the bigger ones I cover with dirt from a mound.
In return, he's now more careful with human bones,
and gives me a warning whistle when he's coming in.
Unfortunately, he doesn't go away
as quickly as he used to. He likes to lean
over a common grave and have his say
on my work. He refers to me as "the gardener,"
tells me my crops should be spread out farther.

5.

Maybe his words have got to me. I know
they shouldn't, but lately I've begun to think
about the Resurrection Day and how
the trumpet will blow and the Eye will blink
and all the bodies will stand up from their graves—
but how, here, packed in so deep and tight?
I'm worried I've made a bad mistake.
It came to me in a dream the other night:
I was underground, I couldn't tell how far.
A cold pair of feet pressed against my cheek.
I tried to dig my way through a ceiling of dirt.
I made a hole above my head, then reached
my hands to pull myself up through the ground,
but a pile of skeletons came crashing down.

6.

At night I set my boots outside my door.
Where they go walking and how they come back
caked with dirt and weighing a double more
than when I took them off, is a riddle I can't crack.
Each morning I put them on and walk closer
to the ground, weighted down, almost sinking.
I go to the graveyard as I've gone before,
hoping the Pestilence has ceased, thinking
today I'll find a priest and not the carter;
I'll be back digging one grave at a time.
I can't imagine this can get much harder
and then it does. It rains or else it rimes;
the carter has come ahead of me and stacked
bodies beside a grave already over-packed.

7.

When does it end?

    When everyone has died.

Who'll bury me?

    No one. You are a grave.

I am a grave?

    And a digger besides.

And those I buried?

    You kept each one of them safe.

Did I know them?

    You imagined you did.

Did I know them?

    More than you can believe.

And will they rise?

    At the end, none shall be hid.

Will they know me?

    As a hole knows a sieve.

I'm not satisfied.

    What was it you wanted?

More, always more.

    When is a grave finally full?

More, always more.

    What was it you wanted?

To look beyond.

    And was your looking full?

It never is.

    But part is better than none.

Except, except

    all that was lost is gone.

Brethren of the Cross: Oxford, May 19, 1349

‿ω‿

> Some element of the flagellant lurked in the
> mind of every medieval man.
>
> *The Black Death*, 64

Although in Wyclif the element was trace,
And not much lurked in his mind without his knowing,
Still he could not look away, and something—
Was it sympathy or kinship?—went out from him
like a bird from its cage.

He stood among the crowd and watched
Over a hundred flagellants
Stripped to the waist, scourges in hand,
Grouped in a circle. Gradually their chanting
Rose in pitch and volume

As they beat their backs and chests
With spikes sewn into leather thongs,
Tearing their flesh, now bleeding
Openly, freely, in front of God, the crowd, and him
On an early afternoon with the shadow

Of St. Mary's spreading across the square,
The tip of its spire pointing
Like a finger at the righteous suffering,
As if to settle all the arguments
Over what would end this Plague:

Here, these few who give themselves
For the many. Wyclif felt their blows
Himself and without thinking
Touched his chest, half expecting blood
To soak through his robe and stain his hand.

But when he took his hand away
And saw nothing, he knew
He had only lapsed into believing.
As suddenly as the cage had opened
It closed. He left without a word.

Ordination

After much talk of duty and dogma
comes the moment to be sealed.
Wyclif stands before the bishop,

bows his head, closes his eyes,
and feels three winds
blow across his face:

one for the Father,
one for the Son,
and one for the Holy Spirit.

In that tempest a city
is destroyed, all its houses
brought down to their foundations

and swept clean away. Only
a bare hill remains
on the space above his brow.

There the bishop builds
the cross, two beams linked
in the place of the skull.

Of all the miracles
Wyclif ever believed,
none taxed him more

than to find himself
still standing with all that weight
on his forehead

as the bishop moved away.

Last Rites

A door opens. Wyclif climbs the stairs
and stands at the bedside
of the dying. He says a prayer,

places the host on a tongue,
and makes the sign of the cross
before leaving. He does the same

at another house on the same street,
then later at a house one street over.
At night when he walks home

he carries the sour smell of their sickness.
No matter where he hangs his cloak,
the last breaths of the dying come off of it

and enter his dreams, turning everything
to rot. When he wakes
he can only remember a force

that made him hold
a piece of straw in one hand
and bless it with the other.

A Young Italian Man Healed of the Plague by
Saint Bridget of Sweden

I could tell you what it's like being dead,
could discourse plainer than the scholars do.
A saint from Sweden laid her hand on my head.

Two days of plague, delirious in bed,
if Mother hadn't prayed to every saint she knew,
I could tell you what it's like being dead.

She called of course on Roch: *Please, please,* she prayed,
oh saint who survived—how we need you.
But it was the saint from Sweden who laid her hand on my head

and with that touch pulled me from what we dread.
I was in a gondola on a dark canal. The wind blew.
If I could, I'd tell you all of what it's like being dead.

The gondolier was hooded. People pled
to him from the banks: *Take me, take me, too!*
But a saint from Sweden laid her hand on my head.

There's more: lanterns on the shore, what the gondolier said.
But I can't guarantee my vision's true.
I would like to tell you what it's like being dead,
but Saint Bridget of Sweden laid her hand on my head.

Ibn Khatir Tells How He Survived the Black Death

Today oranges bloomed
in the courtyard
for the first time in three years
of rain and quakes
and what the doctors called
the judgment of God.

The Plague has taken half our town,
but gone are the days
when goats marched untended
down our streets, nosing a body,
putting a hoof to its chest
as if to rouse a drunkard.

My secret was not to listen
when my friend told me
that the stars answered all our questions.
He died beside his telescope
on a night he'd scribbled
"Saturn, Venus, Mars, aligned."

The next day I fired bricks
in the oven where we bake bread.
My daughter filled a jar with chickpeas,
another with olive oil. My wife folded meat
into cloths soaked in salt.
We lived by living indoors.

A month we spent in darkness.
Carts creaked past trundling
their human load, and the bell
in the square tolled death
all day until the rope broke,
or the bellman gave up.

When we emerged that day in June
horns blew in the square
and women rode the backs of men.
Now, even the butterflies have come back.
They pump their wings
on cypress trees, celebrating survival.

Wyclif's Heart Goes Out to a Widow

At his desk he turns
and through the window
sees her, the young widow
bending and rising, bending
and rising again. She is gathering
twigs and small branches,
and has already
almost more than she can carry.
She bounces lightly
on the soles of her feet, adjusting
the load. With a free hand,
she tucks a loose strand
of hair behind her ear.
Wyclif feels pity
(and something else)
as she disappears
around a corner. For the rest
of that day, he tries to work
but can't. He keeps looking
out the window as shadows
lengthen across the yard
like spilled ink,
like dark, dark hair.

IV

Disputations on Human Love, Bearing Especially on a Certain Widow of Fillingham

Wyclif always impressed his colleagues—even those who most bitterly opposed him—with the sanctity of his personal life. He was evidently a deeply spiritual man, possessed of a profound interior life of devotion and a scrupulous, charitable outward behavior.

DAVID LYLE JEFFREY
The Law of Love: English Spirituality in the Age of Wyclif

QUESTION 1: Whether Optics Explains Sufficiently the Phenomenon of Human Love?

It is sought whether vision and light conspire
to make real the longings of a human heart,
namely my own, hidden as heat from fire,
or rather contained, both the whole and a part.
More plainly it is this: when I see her
midday with sunlight in her hair, the light
and my desire to be the light blur,
so that I seem to touch her with my sight.
But what, then, accounts for the invisible?
At night, I close my eyes to double dark
and thus unseen she's yet more sensible,
more real, an afterimage that burned its mark
and shines behind closed lids, as if she'd touched
me back and wanted to be as close as much.

QUESTION 2: Whether Fondness for Her Hair Should Warn a Priest Who Has Vowed Chastity and Meant It?

There is, to start, the example of our Lord,
who did not despise the woman's hair
but gladly let her long, soft curls pour
onto his feet and said, "I am prepared
hereby for my funeral." He meant he could die
now that her hair had touched him. And note, my friend,
that all our sins would be unsatisfied
had Christ not given in to his own end.
And yet we must admit that He was perfect
as we are not. He stopped her at his feet
and followed a greater passion for all elect.
Would we? Brushed once, there'd be no end of need.
This whole body would shake with wanting more.
Priest would disappear. Widow would turn to whore.

QUESTION 3: Whether Going to Her Door Was Not a Most Stupid, Regrettable Act?

One might, in fact, say it was *caritas*,
charity, since I had come with news
that men would soon be bringing at my request
firewood sufficient for her winter's use.
But when she opened up her door to me
I saw how she was not alone, nor ashamed
to be half-robed. I said I was the priest
and pointed to my window across the lane.
She smiled and said she'd need some minutes more
and motioned to the man who was lying in her bed.
I heard them laughing when she shut the door.
I stood there, dumb, then finally cleared my head
enough to know I wasn't where I should be.
Their laughter doubled as they watched me leave.

QUESTION 4: Whether, Once Wounded by Love, One
Ever Heals Completely?

It's like picking at a scab, this love.
I'm a boy again with crusted skin
on my knee. It's best to let it be, but I shove
my nails underneath, and the pleasure-pain
first shocks, then throbs, then only feels uncovered.
So it is when I hear her singing in the yard.
I know I shouldn't look, but overpowered
I do—I turn—I gaze—quickly but hard.
Then I feel as if I've ripped off all my skin:
behind this desk I'm bones and beating heart—
pitiful, raw, and promising once again
this time's the last. I beg the healing to start,
layer upon layer, until I'm so scabbed over
no one, not even I, can penetrate the cover.

How Wyclif Survived the Long, Hard Winter
of 1363: A Diptych

Not by Bread Alone

It almost seemed enough, even
too much at times
when he brought a loaf
still warm into his rooms
and broke it in his hands.
Steam rose to his face
and he'd laugh spontaneously
as if the hands of a lover
he'd never had and would
never have, reached up
to caress his cheeks.
But as the bread cooled
and next day froze, he knew
he'd held bread without
body. Here in ice
his heresy first formed,
a block of thought
as thick as cathedral stone.

But Also Through the Consolation of Books

He read in bed, with his clothes on,
a fur hat pulled down to his ears,
four blankets on top of him.
Through a complex system
involving his chin and both shoulders
he could turn the pages
without taking his hands
out of the covers. True, at times
the cold did play tricks on him.
Midway through *Confessions*
he thought he heard the Saint's teeth
chattering. One bitter afternoon
as he read Aristotle, a dream
took him south, where the Mediterranean
sun danced on a white beach. Illusions,
he acknowledged, but could not
not welcome the company
of friends to share the cold with.

Wyclif Becomes an Instrument of the Spirit

[T]he humble and obedient man becomes . . . an
instrument of the Spirit.

SAINT JOHN OF DAMASCUS, from the Preface
to *The Fount of Knowledge*

He often prayed for help with what he wrote.
Once he even closed his eyes
and held the pen against the page
waiting for the Spirit's voice
to tell him what to say. Minutes passed.
He heard nothing. When he opened his eyes
ink pooled under his empty pen.
What could Wyclif do but wait
until, humble and obedient, broken
from writing words he hated to see,
he set down his instrument
in order to become one. Then the Spirit
took him up, as if he were a reed-pen,
functional and willing to be used.

V

from THE PRIVATE MEDITATIONS OF
JOHN WYCLIF

Wycliffe's personality remains elusive and in some ways unattractive.
Part of the reason for this is that he is too exclusively known
through his writings, which were nearly all angry
denunciations and refutations.

G.H.W. PARKER
The Morning Star: Wycliffe and the Dawn of the Reformation

On Angels

By now no one cares how many would fit on the head of a pin.
They can always make themselves smaller, or the pin bigger,
and being infinite they have all infinity to play scholastic
games. Meanwhile, they watch us in our lecture hall
and see that our only way to fit another scholar in
is by one of us dying. To this the angels have
only pity. They turn the pin on its head,
and then as many angels as the last
scholar has conjectured climb
up the side. They reach
the tip and dance in
bare feet to bleed
for us. This,
we see,
was al-
ways
the
po-
in
t.

On Celibacy

My neighbor sows his garden
in seed from an open hand.

He straddles a row, bends down,
and drops a speck in the ground.

I watch from my window
and feel my feet sink into

soft soil. My hand opens
on my lap, empty.

On the Virgin Birth

〜⚬〜

And the angel said to her, Nor dread thou not, Mary, for thou
has found grace anent God. Lo, thou shall conceive in womb and
shall bear a Son, and thou shall call him Jesus. . . . And Mary
said to the angel, On what manner shall this thing be done? For
I know not man.

THE GOSPEL OF LUKE, CHAPTER I, from
The Wycliffe New Testament

There is no contradiction in the following:
A virgin conceived and bore a son.
Now the grammarians will say,
if she was a virgin, then she did not conceive;
and, if she did not conceive, then she did not bear.
Through their words they show disdain
for Holy Scripture and pay no attention
to greater minds. Even a cursory reading
of Anselm's *De conceptu virginali*
would reveal the common logic
of infinite terms and make plain the manner
in which we every day conceive of such terms
as for instance that of whiteness
by which we call a white wall white.
So likewise a virgin might conceive
and bear inside her what is above her.
The true miracle lies not in conception
nor in birth, but as always in the act of God
who this one time allowed the thought
of every mother-to-be, to be.

On Inspiration

Like some grand migration
of birds, the words came
and settled on my page.

Then, when I looked up,
a dove perched on my windowsill.
I nodded to it awkwardly

and watched it fly away.
All day I felt
too afraid to read

what I had written.
When the ink dried
I hid the page

beneath other pages, believing
that if I were right
pride would make it

impossible to write again,
and if I were wrong
shame would do the same.

On the Eucharist

The sun casts shadows across my desk,
so the inkwell wears a robe
of the Benedictine order,
and the book on its stand
a long, thin mitre.

Across town, scribes
copy down the words
of my *De eucharistia*,
every stroke of their pens
a whisper that will be heard.

How unfinished it feels
to be finished. Only You, Christ,
could speak those words
while the rest of us
must go on waiting.

VI

～〇〇～

BURNING WYCLIF

It was one of the regular diversions of the orthodox in those days . . . to count up
the heresies of John Wyclif, and, as Thomas Fuller dryly says, they were like
the stones of Salisbury Plain, concerning which there is a proverb
that no two men can count them alike.

LEWIS SERGEANT
John Wyclif: Last of the Schoolmen and
First of the English Reformers

On the Eve of Wyclif's Heresy Trial, the Duke of Lancaster Composes a Double Dactyl Against His Friend's Chief Enemy

Mitre and crozier
Archbishop Courtenay
never leaves home without.
Why take such pains?

Hierocratical
costume conceals from us
crutch he must lean upon,
absence of brains.

The Sense in Which Wyclif Might Be Called a Martyr

Once in a dream his hands were tied
behind the stake, his feet sunk
in firewood. Courtenay appeared
in a mitre as tall as a steeple,

which he tilted back with one hand
and with the other reached underneath
to pull out a matchstick
the size of a crozier. He touched its tip

to the wood, but instead of flames
feathers burst around Wyclif's body.
When they cleared, he saw the Archbishop
on the ground, robes on fire,

his enemy now a flaming wheel
rolling away from him, leaving the earth
scorched for miles. The image that stayed
with Wyclif was a charred road

leading back to him, the unharmed,
and making him the martyr
of would-be martyrs, the spared one
whose lungs nevertheless filled with ashes.

Purvey Translates: *In ipso enim vivimus et movemur et sumus*

꙳

Sometimes the words I translated
translated me, as when
I wrote, "In Him we live
and move and are." For days
I dwelled in that mystery
where all air seemed holy
and fearful. I believed
I was a rip running
through God's body, a tear
that only stopped
when I sat still. Then
at my desk, half in daydream
I felt myself placed
as a word on the page,
and suddenly I saw
the whole of who we are
and how we're bound together—
each one of us a word
in the Word of God,
and our life's goal as simple
as remembering the lines
He first drew us with,
the sound and sense
we made in that language
before languages.

One John Dies, the Other Wakes to Crickets

John Ball slept on the ground
of an old ruin, his head
tucked under his arm
like a bird finding warmth
under its own wing. He dreamed
that there was treasure
buried under his elbow
on the spot where he slept.
He watched men circle him, stomp
the earth with their boots,
until the ground collapsed
and he fell through
into lights the shape of diamonds
against a black backdrop
of an underground sky.

John Wyclif slept with three pillows:
two behind his head
and one as a prop
for his left arm, paralyzed
since the first stroke. He dreamed
that he stood behind a lectern
and read a treatise before a crowded hall
at Oxford. When he looked down
at his papers, they weren't there.
He started to speak—nothing,
as though his words were trapped
behind doors sealed behind other doors,
and then he realized
he wasn't wearing clothes.

Ball felt warm air
drift down to him,
and when he woke
saw the reason: around him
eight men on horseback
less than an arrow's
length away. The horses
flared their nostrils
and breathed on him
the most delicious waking
of his life.

Wyclif woke and heard
crickets outside his living
at Lutterworth, their sawing
away, over and over,
made him think of pen tips
moving across parchment,
the kind of squeaking noise
a quill can make as if
it remembered a life
attached to wings, all the air
to move in, and singing in the treetops.

The men dismounted, laughing,
some carried clubs and
some carried ropes. Ball
did not think, ah, my
executioners, and he
did not think, I have one
arrow left—now quick!
He thought instead of stars
the shape of diamonds
underground or overhead,
either way they aimed him
his dream had promised light.

The Black Friars Beg Wyclif to Recant of His Chief Heresy and Die in Peace: A Triptych

Left Piece	*Hinge*	*Center Piece*	*Hinge*	*Right Piece*
The face of Christ	An in-	Wyclif's chamber	An in-	An open book
above a cloud	terlace	bathed in sunlight	terlace	on a stand
that covers his body	of celest-	in the noon of	of birds	and around it
like a robe, and from	ial bodies:	his waking after	laid beak	a circle of
the cloud, loaves	crescent	the second stroke.	to foot	people en-
of bread rain down	moons	He lies in bed,	foot to	circled by
past his bare feet	and	his white beard	beak,	more people
with their round	inside	across the blue	each with	encircled by
wounds dripping	of them	blanket, his eyes	one black	still more—all
blood that streaks	suns	wide open, turned	eye open,	of their eyes
like the residue	with	toward four men	unsmiling.	turned toward
of shooting stars.	faces,	in black robes	Across	the book. They
Below him, priests	followed	standing by the bed	their	are naked, their
raise gold chalices	by orbs	with hands folded	bodies	bodies sketchy
to catch the blood,	painted	in prayer. The one	a white	as if the artist
tonsured monks	silver,	with his hood up	banner	whose job was
hold out their arms	red,	turns his head	with	to finish painting
for the falling bread,	ochre	in the direction of	red	had died of plague
and in a straight line	and lapis	a scribe who stands	words	and the patron
fading to infinity	lazuli.	at the door holding	pro-	would not wait
the parishioners	The	quill and parchment	claims,	for the next
stand waiting with	heavens	preparing to write	*Sola*	artist to appear
their hands cupped	as seen	the heretic's words	*Script-*	so took the piece
and heads bowed.	vertically.	of final confession.	*ura.*	as is and left.

Purvey Describes His Work with Wyclif

Those afternoons in the rectory
seated at opposite sides
of the same table, sunlight
on our manuscripts, an inkwell
shared in the middle, I never
wrote one word for him.
Palsied as he was, the Lord
left his right side unharmed.
In fact, I sometimes thought
the strength he lost in one arm
was transferred to the other.
To see him rush words onto the page!
I thought of squirrels gathering nuts
frantic in October. But he was
pouring out every word he had
knowing his own winter had come.
One time I looked up and saw
his left arm dangling
off the edge of the table, limp
as a tree limb broken
in storm. Quietly, I stood,
walked around the table,
and set his arm back
on the surface. He never stopped writing
or even glanced up at me.
And now as some have begun
to say a sick man could not
have written all we say he did,
I wish to make clear
he did. My only aid was
this simple act of kindness:
I carried a part he no longer
needed. I did not interrupt him
when he worked.

Burning Wyclif

Sometimes you have to raise the body up
to burn it down. So it was with Wyclif,
who rested forty-two years under chancel stone
condemned by the Papacy, protected by the Crown.
Finally, a bishop came with a few men,
spades, shovels, a horse and cart. By then,
not much was left of Wyclif—hair and skin gone,
his bones slipped out of place inside the simple alb
they'd buried him in. The bishop gathered what he could.
Beside the River Swift, he lit a pile of wood
and tossed the bones on one at a time,
cursing the heretic from limb to limb.
Afterwards, they shoveled ash into the water
and no one even thought the word *martyr*.

VII

〜

A Visit to Lutterworth

The difficulty in all brief characterization of Wyclif lies in the fact . . . that Wyclif is
representative of both the medieval and modern world, and that the words which
would truly describe him in the one sphere fail to apply in the other.

HERBERT WORKMAN
*John Wyclif: A Study of the English
Medieval Church*

A Visit to Lutterworth

1.

On a chain-link fence outside the city limits
a sign handwritten on a piece of cardboard:
"Any person who cuts the manes or tails
of these horses shall be prosecuted."

It was after one in the morning. We had stopped
to check the map on our way to Wyclif's church
when our headlights fell on this warning.
In the quiet car, with only the courtesy light on,

Kathy spoke her first thoughts of Lutterworth:
"This place is evil." Somewhere
in that field we couldn't see
horses slept with one eye open

and one nostril flared to scare marauders,
while the farmer sat in his kitchen
with the light on, his coat on a hook,
and his boots pointed like double barrels at the door.

2.

We tried but couldn't find the church
that night. Instead we found a group of men
loud, drunk, stumbling on the main street.
One held another's head

pinched between his arm, and someone shouted,
"Hit him! Hit him!" We agreed
not to ask them for directions
to the church. Back at our B&B,

one press of a button opened the gates.
We drove through, our tires crunching gravel
and stirring two horses, who turned their heads
and watched us through their stable doors.

3.
I thought I knew Wyclif's church
from pictures on the Internet. It has gravestones
leaning over, almost falling, as if the dead
who don't pay rent, but can't be evicted

are doomed to watch their homes collapse
slowly on top of them. I didn't know
that every church in England has the same stones
and the same unflinching landlord.

And so we waited in front of the wrong church
for twenty minutes before we realized
we waited in front of the wrong church. It took
directions from a paper boy, an illegal turn,

and a side gate that mercifully wasn't locked
for us to make it in time for the service.

4.
We entered through a heavy wooden door.
Inside was silence and stone walls
set in place seven centuries ago.
A man gave us programs and pointed

to the smaller sanctuary, just beyond
a fresco of the Doomsday.
We only had to look up to see the dead
come out of their graves,

some with one foot still in the ground.
Above them, Christ sat on a rainbow-bridge,
his bare and still-wounded feet
dangling over the edge.

5.
I knelt for the Prayers of the People.
It must have been the Rector's voice
or jet lag that made me imagine
my pew lurched forward

and hovered over the chancel
where Wyclif had been buried.
But I could also believe in bones,
even a chip or trace

left behind when the Bishop's men
dug Wyclif up, tossed his remains
on a wagon and drove off
to the River Swift.

Whatever moved me felt real
as a dream, and brought me
the closest I've ever come
to communing with the dead.

6.
After the service, small talk.
Where we're from and why we've come.
From Indiana. For research.
The Rector and my wife find common ground

in Colombia and the story of missionaries
kidnapped and killed. It takes the smallest crack

and the dead enter our conversation,
like that other fresco, the one we didn't see

coming in, but looms over us now:
"The Three Living and the Three Dead"
it's called, from a French legend
where three kings encounter

three skeletons. "We were once
as you are now," the skeletons say
and the kings flee. Their words
hang in the air above our words.

I listen and nod.

The Caretaker of St. Mary's Church Comments on Recent Scholarly Findings

We never claimed to have John Wyclif's bones
inside our church these last six hundred years.
What we believed is now but once supposed.

A bishop took and burned them so long ago
none now can trace back to an ancestor.
So we never claimed to have John Wyclif's bones.

But now the experts have come and we are told
our plaques are false. They say that's not his chair.
What we believed is now but once supposed.

Nor is this his pulpit, though our priest intoned
the famous name and said he once stood there.
Still, he never claimed we had John Wyclif's bones.

We did believe we had his ancient cloak,
and kept it sealed in glass on this wall here.
What we believed is now but once supposed.

But when they broke the glass to have their proof
the cloth disintegrated, exposed to air.
Good thing we never claimed to have his bones,
else Wyclif, too, would be but once supposed.

Snowbound in Wickliffe, Ohio

Nightfall and the interstate covered
with new snow, we knew we couldn't make it
all the way home without rest, so pulled off
(of all places!) in Wickliffe, Ohio.

How could I not think of poems
and imagine a link even here,
as if the Midwest and the Middle Ages,
convenience store gas stations and St. Mary's Cathedral

belonged together, separated by only
a half dozen centuries as thin as paper?
Even the desk clerk reminded me
of certain portraits I've seen of Wyclif.

And when I walked to our room
I couldn't help looking around the parking lot
for a bent man with a gray beard,
approximately six hundred and eighty years old.

That night I slept within the limits of my subject,
and when I woke couldn't remember my dreams.
The snow that covered Wickliffe covered me, too,
holding us both at its mercy before letting us go.

Notes

⌤

JOHN WYCLIF (ca. 1324–1384) was born and raised in Northern England, perhaps near Richmond in Yorkshire. He attended and later taught at Oxford, becoming the University's most renowned scholar during the latter half of the fourteenth century. His years coincided with the Black Death (1347–1350), a Papal Schism (begun in 1378), and the Peasants' Revolt (1381). His writings and lectures inspired the first complete translation of the Bible into English and involved him in life-threatening controversies with Church authorities. Pope Gregory XI and Archbishop William Courtenay both condemned him.

Habitus: "Doctor Evangelicus" is a derogatory term used by Wyclif's enemies. It referred to his unusual practice of quoting extensively and frequently from the four gospels in his scholarly work. "Morning Star" is a more positive term used by his supporters. It indicates Wyclif's role as a forerunner to the Protestant Reformation.

Awake in Oxford: Balliol was a hall at Oxford during Wyclif's lifetime and remains so today, although the original structure has been lost.

Tonsure: It is uncertain whether Wyclif wore a tonsure during his student days. Some biographers believe he must have, while others (notably Herbert Workman in *John Wyclif: A Study of the English Medieval Church*) disagree.

The Steward's Prayer Book: An account of Christ healing the ten lepers appears in Luke 17: 11–19.

William of Ockham Visits the Sick: Franciscan theologian William of Ockham (1285–1347) is sometimes numbered among Wyclif's teachers at Oxford.

Brethren of the Cross: Oxford, May 19, 1349: The Flagellants were an extreme sect of Christians who believed that through self-inflicted punishment, as described in this poem, they could appease God for the sins that had brought on the plague. They traveled to major cities and paraded before the people, often around a cathedral. Although there is no record of the Flagellants appearing in Oxford on this date, they did visit London at around this time.

A Young Italian Man Healed of the Plague . . . : Philip Ziegler in *The Black Death* records the event as follows: "Saint Bridget was among the visitors [to Rome] arriving early in 1349. . . . One male Orsini, it is recorded, had caught the plague and was despaired of by the doctors. 'If only the Lady Bridget were here!' sighed his mother. 'Her touch would cure my son.' At that moment in walked the saint. She prayed by the invalid's bedside, laid her hand on his forehead and left him, a few hours later fully restored to health." Saint Roch (ca. 1295–ca. 1327) survived his own bout with the plague and was believed to have the power to heal plague victims who called on his name.

Ibn Khatir Tells How He Survived the Black Death: Ziegler cites a similar story (*Black Death* 38) concerning Ibn Abu Madyan. The name Ibn Khatir is made up.

Wyclif's Heart Goes Out to a Widow: This poem and the first four poems in section IV are set in Fillingham, England, where Wyclif served as vicar beginning in 1361.

How Wyclif Survived the Long, Hard Winter . . . : A diptych is a two-paneled altar piece, usually of wood. Herbert Workman says this about the winter of 1363: "Wyclif [was] at Oxford in the severe winter of 1363 when a great frost lasted from 30th November until the 19th March 1364. The sufferings involved in the comfortless, fireless rooms of medieval Oxford can be imagined when we remember that during that winter the Rhone froze at Avignon and the Meuse at Liège."

On the Eucharist: Wyclif's denial of transubstantiation represents, to his contemporaries, his most serious heresy. His views on the Eucharist were formally worked out in *De eucharistia* (1379) and have been summarized by Ian Christopher Levy in this way: "Following the consecration of the host . . . the bread demonstrated in the proposition 'This is my body' still remains bread while at the same time is admitted to be the body of Christ. . . . Here Christ was employing a manner of speaking often found within Scripture, one intended to convey that the bread efficaciously and sacramentally signifies his body." (Introduction, *On the Truth of Holy Scripture* 28–29).

On the Eve of Wyclif's Heresy Trial . . . : The Duke of Lancaster (1340–1399) was the fourth son of King Edward III and first met Wyclif as early as 1374, employing him in political service in 1376.

Purvey Translates . . . After Wyclif was expelled from his post at Oxford, John Purvey followed him to Lutterworth and served as his personal secretary and assistant. The case has grown strong for believing that Purvey, not Wyclif, deserves credit for completing the first full translation of the Bible into English, an act for which he was imprisoned. Records show that Purvey was still in prison in 1421, but we do not know when or where he died.

One John Dies, the Other Wakes to Crickets: John Ball (d. 1381) was one of the leaders of the Peasants' Revolt and executed for his part in the uprising. Recent scholarship makes plain that Ball and Wyclif did not work together, as had earlier been thought. Wyclif's own involvement in the events is best seen as indirect, perhaps as a catalyst through his writings, which often call for a radical redistribution of wealth. Wyclif believed, for instance, that the clergy should voluntarily relinquish their worldly goods and live in evangelical poverty.

The Black Friars Beg Wyclif . . . : The Black Friars belonged to the Benedictine order and could be distinguished by their long black robes.

Burning Wyclif: The events described here occurred in the spring of 1428. The bishop who carried out the order to disinter, burn, and scatter Wyclif's remains was Richard Fleming. The River Swift is in Lutterworth, a short walk from St. Mary's church.

Selected by Robert Fink, *Burning Wyclif* is the fifteenth winner of the
Walt McDonald First-Book Competition in Poetry. The competition
is supported generously through donated subscriptions
from *The American Scholar, The Atlantic Monthly,*
The Georgia Review, Gulf Coast,
The Hudson Review,
The Massachusetts Review,
Poetry, Shenandoah,
and
The Southern Review.